Language Around the World

WRITTEN BY GILL BUDGELL

ILLUSTRATED BY KATY HALFORD

Penguin
Random
House

Author Gill Budgell
Illustrator Katy Halford

Created and designed for DK by **Plum5 Ltd**

Publishing Project Manager Katherine Neep
Product Manager Sarah Forbes
Production Controller Isabell Schart
Senior Picture Researcher Sumedha Chopra
Production Editor Shanker Prasad
Consultants EL Education
Copy Editor Allison Singer
DE&I Editor Claire Philip

First American Edition, 2023
Published in the United States by DK Publishing
1745 Broadway, 20th Floor, New York, NY 10019

Copyright © 2023 Dorling Kindersley Limited
DK, a Division of Penguin Random House LLC
23 24 25 10 9 8 7 6 5 4 3 2
002–335440 –Aug/2023

A catalog record for this book
is available from the Library of Congress.
ISBN 978-0-7440-8006-3

DK books are available at special discounts when purchased
in bulk for sales promotions, premiums, fund-raising, or educational use.
For details, contact: DK Publishing Special Markets,
1745 Broadway, 20th Floor, New York, NY 10019
SpecialSales@dk.com

Printed and bound in China

The publisher would like to thank the following for their
kind permission to reproduce their photographs:

(Key: a-above; b-below/bottom; c-centre; f-far; l-left; r-right; t-top)

10 Dreamstime.com: Tom Wang (cl). **14 Alamy Stock Photo:**
BSIP SA. **16 Dorling Kindersley:** Bolton Library and Museum
Services (clb). **17 123RF.com:** serge75 (tc). **Alamy Stock
Photo:** Abaca Press (clb). **28 Alamy Stock Photo:** Granger
- Historical Picture Archive (cl). **29 Alamy Stock Photo:** The
History Collection (tr); Pictorial Press Ltd (c). **33 Getty Images
/ iStock:** Feverpitched (tl). **34 Getty Images:** Roderick Chen /
Photodisc (cl). **35 Getty Images:** Suman Kumar / EyeEm (tc).
Robert Harding Picture Library: Sean Sprague (cr). **39 Alamy
Stock Photo:** Prisma Archivo (br). **42 Dorling Kindersley:**
The Flag Institute (c); The Flag Institute (clb). **44 Alamy Stock
Photo:** Granger - Historical Picture Archive (bc).
45 Alamy Stock Photo: The History Collection (cla); Pictorial
Press Ltd (tc)

All other images © Dorling Kindersley

For further information see: www.dkimages.com

For the curious
www.dk.com

MIX
Paper | Supporting
responsible forestry
FSC™ C018179

This book was made with Forest
Stewardship Council™ certified
paper - one small step in DK's
commitment to a sustainable future.
For more information go to
www.dk.com/our-green-pledge

CONTENTS

WHAT IS LANGUAGE?

Language is how people communicate, or share ideas and information. It is usually spoken and written. Some languages are only spoken because there is no agreed way to write the letters and sounds. One example is Pirahã, which is spoken by the Pirahã people of Brazil, South America.

Some languages are signed mainly using hand gestures. The signing is used by and with people who are deaf or hard of hearing, or who cannot speak.

Some languages are written using braille. Braille is a system of reading and writing that uses touch. It is used by and with people who are blind or cannot see well.

People have different languages for different purposes. Language helps us share knowledge, tell stories, and explain how we feel or what we are thinking.

Some people use many languages. We say they are **multilingual**. *Multi* means *many*.

Some people use two languages. We say they are **bilingual**. *Bi* means *two*.

Hallo!
(hal-low)

Jambo!
(jam-bow)

Olá
(o-lah)

Hi!

Hej!
(hi)

Ciao!
(chow)

SIGN LANGUAGE

BRAILLE

There are more than seven thousand languages across the world. This number changes over time as new languages develop and old languages become extinct when people stop using them.

Different countries often have one or two official languages, but people within the country may speak many other languages too. For example, experts think that people use as many as 430 different languages in the United States of America.

The same language can sound different when spoken by different people. Different languages sound different. Languages can look different when written too.

THE SIX MOST COMMONLY SPOKEN LANGUAGES IN THE WORLD

ENGLISH
(the most common language among multilingual speakers)

Hello! (hell-low)

MANDARIN CHINESE

Nǐhǎo! (nee-how)

HINDI

Namaste! (nuh-muh-stay)

SPANISH

Hola! (oh-lah)

FRENCH

Bonjour! (bon-zhoor)

STANDARD ARABIC

Marhaban! (mar-har-ban)

LET'S COMMUNICATE!

People can communicate in different ways, but we mostly speak, listen, read, and write languages.

Try recording yourself speaking at different volumes and in different tones to hear how they can seem to change the meaning of what you are saying.

SPEAKING

Speaking is one of the main ways that people can use language to communicate. To speak effectively, you should think about these things:

- Look at the person or people to whom you are speaking.
- Speak clearly.
- Choose the best words for your audience.
- Decide which volume and tone you will use when speaking the words.

Speak loudly if you want to grab people's attention!

Volume is about how loudly you are speaking.

Tone is about the way you say something. Tone can change the meaning. It's not just what you say, but how you say it!

READING

Different languages use the same or similar letters to represent sounds. We have to learn the letter shapes and sounds in order to be able to read the words. Being able to read is an important part of using a language in its written form. We read for information, and we read for enjoyment.

LISTENING

Listening is the opposite and equal side of speaking.
To listen effectively, you should think about these things:

- Sit still, and look at the speaker.
- Nod or shake your head to show you are concentrating.
- Try to understand the speaker's point of view.
- Do not interrupt.

WRITING

Just like for reading, we need to learn the letter shapes and sounds for writing. Writing helps us organize our thoughts, share information, and communicate with others.

Being fluent in a language means you understand it very well—and that others understand you. You are able to speak, listen, read, and/or write it clearly.
Having one or two of these skills in any language, is valuable for communication.

LETTERS, SOUNDS, AND SYMBOLS

Different languages have different sounds and symbols to stand for letters or words.

LETTERS AND SOUNDS

The English alphabet has 26 letters. Letters are symbols. Twenty letters are consonants, and five letters are vowels. The letter Y can be a consonant or a vowel as in **yak** and **Egypt**. The 26 letters can be mixed up to stand for about 44 sounds. The sounds can be used in about 128 different ways to spell words.

안녕

Сайн уу

Annyeong
Korean

Sain uu
Mongolian

But not all alphabets have the same number of letters and sounds. Look at page 42 to find out about the longest and shortest alphabets!

And not all alphabets have letters that stand for the same kind of sounds.

A group of languages mostly spoken in southern Africa use clicking sounds. Some languages around the world use whistling sounds.

tsk-tsk

tut-tut

Z Y X W V U T S R Q P O N M L K J I H G F E D C B A

SYMBOLS

Alphabets can look very different from one another too. The ancient Egyptian alphabet was made up of symbols, or pictures called hieroglyphs.

This is the hieroglyph.

This is roughly the sound the hieroglyph makes.

This is what the hieroglyph represents.

Most of the hieroglyphs stand for the name of something and for a letter sound. In Egyptian, the cobra stands for the sound made by the letter J.

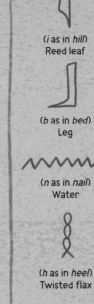

(*a* as in *hat*)
Egyptian vulture

(*oo* as in *too* or *w* as in *wind*)
Quail chick

(*m* as in *man*)
Owl

(*h* as in *house*)
House

(*i* as in *hill*)
Reed leaf

(*b* as in *bed*)
Leg

(*n* as in *nail*)
Water

(*h* as in *heel*)
Twisted flax

(*s* as in *sun*)
Door bolt

(*c* as in *cat*)
Basket

(*tch* as in *itch*)
Tethering rope

(*y* as in *happy*)
Double reed leaf

(*p* as in *pen*)
Box

(*r* as in *rope*)
Mouth

(*ch* as in *loch*)
We don't know!

(*sh* as in *sheep*)
Pool

(*g* as in *garden*)
Jar stand

(*d* as in *dog*)
Hand

(*e* as in *pet*)
Arm

(*f* as in *finger* or *v* as in *vet*)
Horned viper

(*l* as in *light*)
Lion

(*kh* as in *ankh*)
Animal belly

(*k* as in *kick* or *q* as in *queen*)
Hill slope

(*t* as in *time*)
Loaf of bread

(*j* as in *jam*)
Cobra

Kan ji

漢字

Hi ra ga na

ひらがな

Ka ta ka na

カタカナ

In Japan, there are three different alphabets. Kanji has a few thousand symbols. Hiragana and Katakana have 46 symbols each.

The symbols in each alphabet look very different, and you have to learn when to use each one. That's a lot to learn!

9

BODY LANGUAGE

You can use your hands, face, and body to help with communication. Some experts say that your body language is as important as the words you use or the tone of your voice.

HANDS

People often use their hands while they talk.
You can use your hands without words to communicate.

Many people around the world make a heart shape to share a message of love.

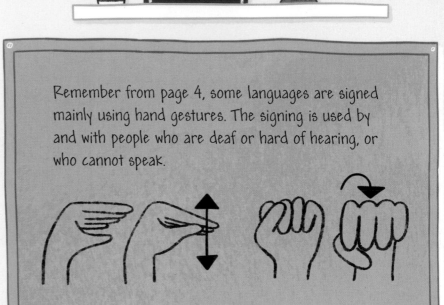

Remember from page 4, some languages are signed mainly using hand gestures. The signing is used by and with people who are deaf or hard of hearing, or who cannot speak.

No in American Sign Language

Yes in American Sign Language

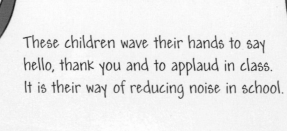

These children wave their hands to say hello, thank you and to applaud in class. It is their way of reducing noise in school.

FACE
Looking at someone's face may tell you how they are feeling.

Raising your eyebrows can show surprise.

Wrinkling your nose can show dislike.

Smiling can show happiness.

BODY
The way you use and move your body can show how you are feeling. Nodding your head may show agreement. Shaking your head may show disagreement. Crossing your arms in front of your chest may show you are frustrated or closed to ideas. Opening your arms wide may show you are welcoming or that you feel strongly about what you are saying.

But be careful! Some body language means different things in different countries. In some countries a gesture might mean *OK* or *come here*, but in another country it might mean something rude!

BABY TALK

How do babies learn to talk?

Experts ask big, important questions like this one. They research for a long time to find the answers, but the answers are not always easy to find. We don't yet know for sure how babies learn to talk!

Babies' bodies grow fast. Their brains develop quickly too.

Some experts think babies are born with a skill to explore language in order to learn to talk.

Some experts think babies are born with a skill to follow a set pathway in the brain in order to learn to talk.

And other experts think babies are born with the skill to copy what they hear in order to learn to talk.

One thing is for sure: babies learn by experimenting and making mistakes, just as we all do our whole lives.

CHIT CHAT

At around 12 months, babies start trying to speak their first words. By age two, they can generally use between 50 and 100 words. By age three, some children can use more than 1,000 words.

8 TO 20 WEEKS
Babies coo and laugh.

Coo

20 TO 30 WEEKS
Babies play with their voice. They make high and low sounds. They make long sounds. They make funny sounds!

Squeeeal Ah-yoo

30 TO 50 WEEKS
Babies babble. Babbling sounds are not necessarily like the language they will speak.

Ga-ga-gah

Wa-wa-wa

9 TO 18 MONTHS
Babies make clear sounds that begin to sound like the language they will speak.

Eh-oh

Doggy

Some children take much longer to learn to speak than others, and not all people end up speaking verbally. Find out more about this on pages 4 and 5, and pages 10 and 11.

LANGUAGE LEARNERS FOR LIFE

The brain is the control center of your body. It helps you think and do all kinds of amazing things. One of those amazing things is learning language.

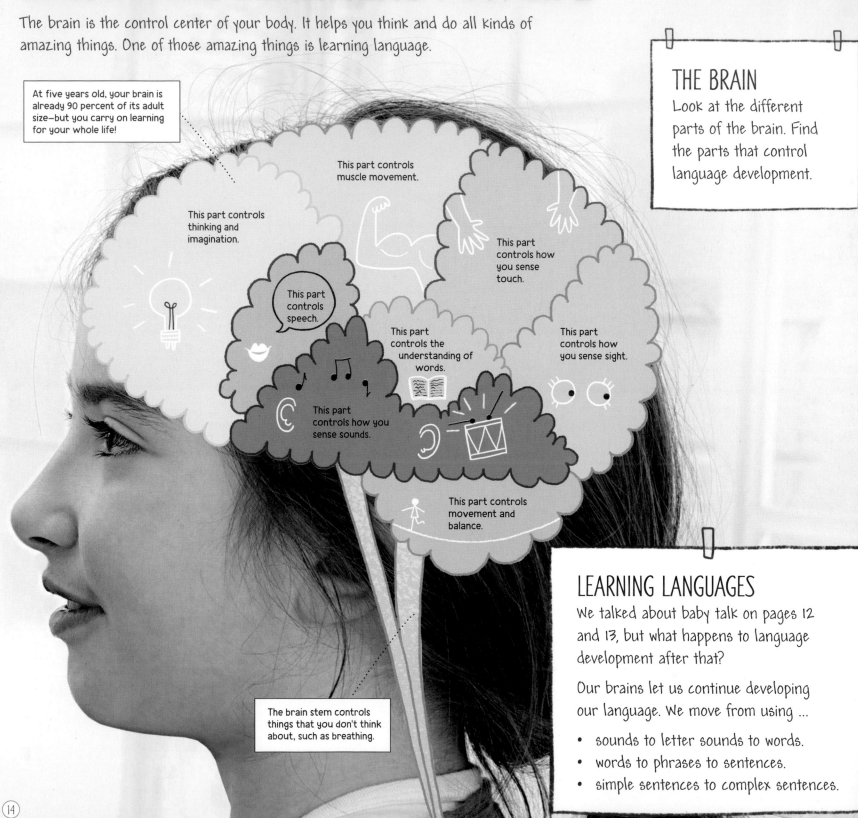

At five years old, your brain is already 90 percent of its adult size—but you carry on learning for your whole life!

This part controls thinking and imagination.

This part controls muscle movement.

This part controls speech.

This part controls how you sense touch.

This part controls the understanding of words.

This part controls how you sense sight.

This part controls how you sense sounds.

This part controls movement and balance.

The brain stem controls things that you don't think about, such as breathing.

THE BRAIN
Look at the different parts of the brain. Find the parts that control language development.

LEARNING LANGUAGES
We talked about baby talk on pages 12 and 13, but what happens to language development after that?

Our brains let us continue developing our language. We move from using ...

- sounds to letter sounds to words.
- words to phrases to sentences.
- simple sentences to complex sentences.

AT THE PARK

There are lots of things to see and do in the park.

p is for *park*

How do you say *dog* in German?

Hund

weeeee!

SLIDE

The park is ... grassy, leafy, airy.

MEET FRIENDS

We learn to use language in social settings with others. We learn most of these things while we are school age.

But our understanding of language develops throughout our lives. And we may use what we know in one language to learn other languages too.

ANCIENT LANGUAGES

Humans have been using some form of language for thousands of years. Languages grow and evolve over time. Some ancient, or very old, languages are still used today. They are a reflection of the past as well as the present. Which of the world's ancient languages are still spoken today?

EGYPTIAN: About 4,700 years old. It is from and used in the north of East Africa. We no longer see hieroglyphs, but the language still used today is called Coptic. It is mainly used in religious texts.

SANSKRIT: About 3,500 years old. It is mainly used in religious texts. You can still study Sanskrit at colleges and universities. Many people speak it as a second language.

CHINESE: About 3,300 years old, but some experts think it is even older. For sure, it is one of the oldest written and spoken ancient languages. There are many different forms of Chinese today, but Mandarin and Cantonese are two that are still widely used and descended from ancient Chinese.

3,500

3,300

4,700

GREEK: About 3,500 years old. It is still spoken as a main, everyday first language, but modern Greek has changed a lot from ancient Greek.

ARAMAIC: About 3,100 years old. It is older than both Hebrew and Arabic, but in the same language family. It is still spoken by up to one million people in the world today.

2,500

FARSI: About 2,500 years old. Today there are about 110 million speakers of Farsi around the world.

Ancient Hebrew scroll

3,100

HEBREW: About 3,000 years old. Today there are about nine million speakers of modern Hebrew.

Aramaic statue

3,000

FUN FACT

The way all languages are interconnected and the way they evolve makes it difficult to give hard-and-fast start and end dates or an official age.

We do know that most languages were spoken for a long time before they were ever written down. This means most languages are older than the historical records we have for them.

WORLD LANGUAGE FAMILIES

A language family is a group of different languages that all develop from one other common language. Most languages spoken in the world belong to a language family.

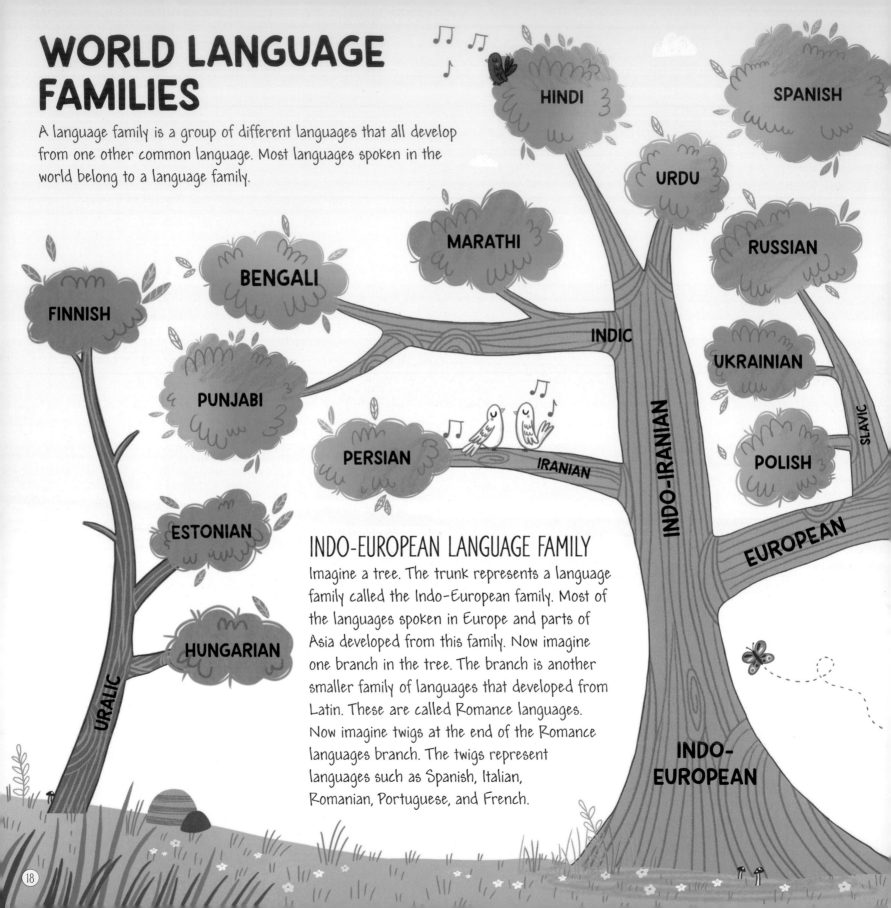

HINDI

SPANISH

URDU

MARATHI

BENGALI

RUSSIAN

FINNISH

INDIC

PUNJABI

UKRAINIAN

PERSIAN

IRANIAN

INDO-IRANIAN

SLAVIC

POLISH

ESTONIAN

EUROPEAN

INDO-EUROPEAN LANGUAGE FAMILY

Imagine a tree. The trunk represents a language family called the Indo-European family. Most of the languages spoken in Europe and parts of Asia developed from this family. Now imagine one branch in the tree. The branch is another smaller family of languages that developed from Latin. These are called Romance languages. Now imagine twigs at the end of the Romance languages branch. The twigs represent languages such as Spanish, Italian, Romanian, Portuguese, and French.

HUNGARIAN

URALIC

INDO-EUROPEAN

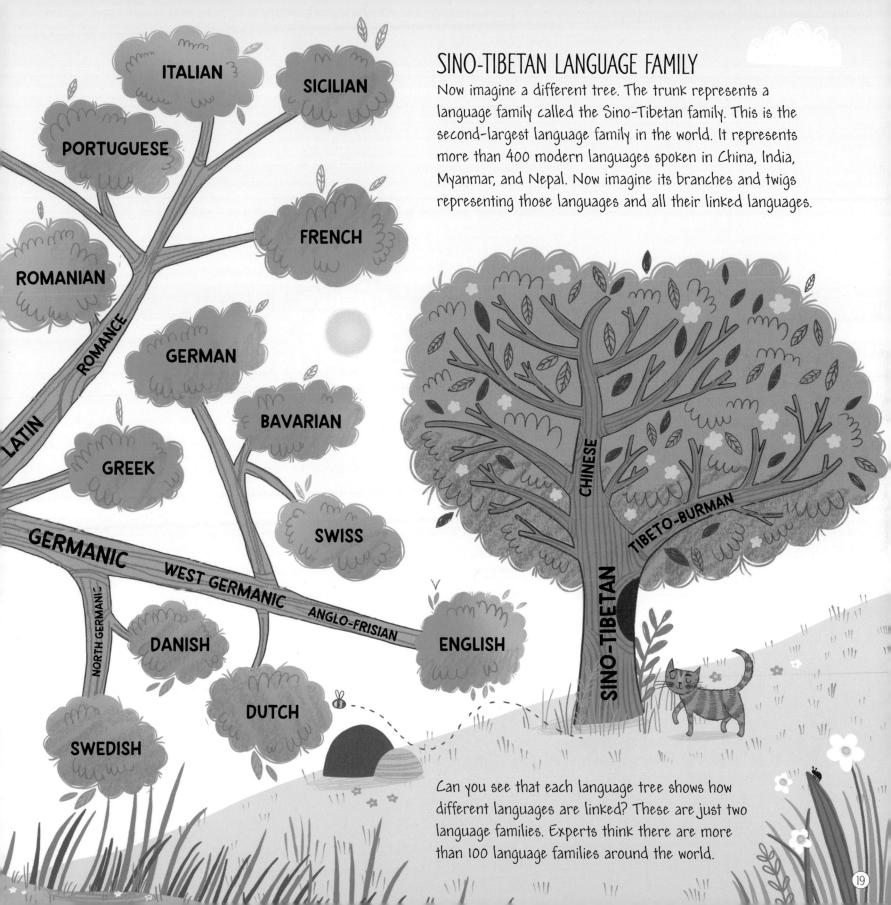

ITALIAN

SICILIAN

PORTUGUESE

FRENCH

ROMANIAN

ROMANCE

GERMAN

LATIN

BAVARIAN

GREEK

SWISS

GERMANIC

WEST GERMANIC

ANGLO-FRISIAN

NORTH GERMANIC

DANISH

ENGLISH

DUTCH

SWEDISH

SINO-TIBETAN LANGUAGE FAMILY

Now imagine a different tree. The trunk represents a language family called the Sino-Tibetan family. This is the second-largest language family in the world. It represents more than 400 modern languages spoken in China, India, Myanmar, and Nepal. Now imagine its branches and twigs representing those languages and all their linked languages.

CHINESE

TIBETO-BURMAN

SINO-TIBETAN

Can you see that each language tree shows how different languages are linked? These are just two language families. Experts think there are more than 100 language families around the world.

WHY AND HOW DOES LANGUAGE CHANGE?

Experts think there is no single reason for language change. People move from place to place to work, share ideas, find a better place to live, and experience new cultures. They bring their food, books, religions, and traditions. The language for all of these things travels with the people.

LET'S LOOK AT AN EXAMPLE FROM THE PAST

The Vikings lived a long time ago in northern Europe. Their name means *raider*, and they traveled to find new lands and raid the treasures of those living there.

They sailed along the rivers of Russia to the Black Sea and out into the North Sea and North Atlantic to work, live, learn, and eat.

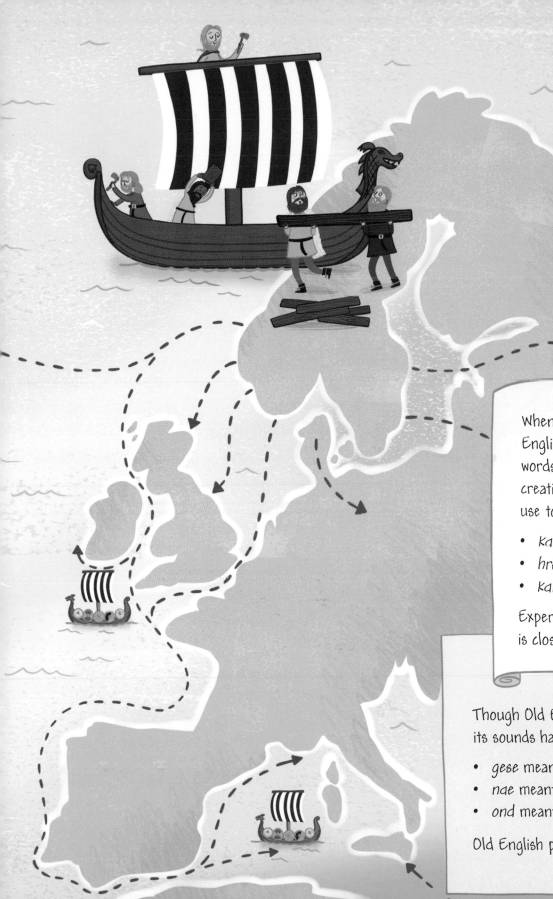

FACT FILE

WHO: The Vikings

LANGUAGE: Old Norse

WHEN: The Middle Ages, between about 790 and 1050

WHERE FROM: Originally in Denmark, Sweden, and Norway

WHERE TO: Britain, Ireland, France, Iceland, Greenland, and North America

When they invaded Britain, people there spoke Old English. The Vikings spoke Old Norse. Over time, words from Old Norse mixed with Old English, creating a new variation of English. Many words we use today come from Old Norse. For example:

- *kaka* meant *cake*.
- *hreindyri* meant *reindeer*.
- *kalla* meant *to call*.

Experts say that the language spoken in Iceland today is closest to the Old Norse used by the Vikings.

Though Old English is no longer spoken, some of its sounds have survived. In the tenth century:

- *gese* meant *yes*.
- *nae* meant *no*.
- *ond* meant *and*.

Old English pronouns like *we* and *he* are still in use today.

PEOPLE ON THE MOVE IN MODERN TIMES

Language represents people and moves with people. Remember how the Vikings brought Old Norse to Old English? It's the same today when people travel to live in a different country. They may learn the language of their new country, but they bring a language with them to use with family and friends in their community. As the languages are shared, they change.

Food is important to all people. When people move around the world, they still want to cook and eat the food of their country. As those foods become popular, the names become more common.

You may not speak Spanish.
But do you know these words?

- banana
- taco
- burrito
- chorizo

It's not a fiesta without food, and all that food adds up to a fiesta!

You may not speak Italian.
But do you know these words?

- pizza
- pasta
- gelato
- pesto

Panini without mozzarella is a fiasco!

You may not speak any Indian languages.
But do you know these words?

- aloo gobi
- chicken tikka masala
- samosa
- biryani

Bhel puri with chutney is a tasty Indian snack!

This doesn't mean that food is the only thing that changes language, but in a small way, it helps.

Think about the words you know that may have come from a different language.

USE YOUR LANGUAGE OR LOSE IT

Languages are alive! But they can only survive if they are used and passed from one generation to another. If they are not used or only a few people are using a language, it becomes endangered. If no one is using a language or passing it on, then it dies. It becomes a dead, or extinct, language.

Latin was once spoken in the Roman Empire. It's now a dead language.

However, you can still choose to learn it at some schools, colleges, and universities.

And many modern languages, such as Portuguese, French, Italian, and Spanish, developed from it.

Some Latin words link and translate to English words.

LATIN	LINKED ENGLISH WORD	ENGLISH TRANSLATION
murus	mural	wall
hortus	horticulture	garden
liber	library	book
mare	marine	sea

Most of the languages spoken by the original people who lived in North America are now endangered. Five of those languages have become extinct in the last one hundred years.

One of those languages is Serrano. Serrano was spoken by the indigenous people of Southern California.

In the past, many of these indigenous people were misled to believe that speaking English would give them a better life, so they stopped speaking their own languages.

Julie Flett is a Cree-Métis author and illustrator of children's books. The Métis are an indigenous group of people in Canada. One of the languages they may speak is sometimes called French Cree. It is considered an endangered language.

Julie writes her books in English and Cree to share her language and culture, and to keep them alive.

ALOHA!

Did you know that you can learn some endangered languages, such as Navajo, Hawaiian, and Irish, using online language programs?

25

ALL LANGUAGES ARE MEANINGFUL

No one language is better than another, and all languages are meaningful. You just have to explore the language to find the meaning! Learning languages can be good for our brains.

HOW MANY LANGUAGES?

The language we learn from our parents is our first or home language. But many people use two or more languages at home and in the community. Remember from page 4, if you know two languages, you are bilingual. If you know many languages, you are multilingual.

Hello

Kia Ora
(ki ao-ra)

Bi means *two* in Latin. *Multi* means *many*.

What languages are used in your home or community?

ARIA is ten years old. She lives on New Zealand's North Island and is Māori. She attends a bilingual school that teaches both Te Reo Māori and English. The Māori were the first people to live on New Zealand.

Learning another language can help you become a better communicator and see the world in a different way. Read the poem "Double Fun" to see how this may be true.

Porque hablo ingles y español …

DOUBLE FUN

JULIO

Because I speak English and Spanish

I can sit by my **grandma**–*abuela* and tell her about school.

We talk about **books** or *libros*, **maths** or *matemáticas*, and **friends** or *amigos*.

GIANNA

Because I speak English and Italian

I can enjoy the stories my **mom**–*mamma* reads me at night

I say **thanks** or *grazie*, **sleepy** or *assonnata*, and **good night** or *buona notte*!

STEPH

Because I speak English and Greek

I watch soccer with my **dad**–μπαμπάς *(bampás)*

We shout **goal** or στόχος *(stóchos)*,
super team or σούπερ ομάδα *(soúper omáda)*,
and **champions** or πρωταθλητές *(protathlités)*!

Because we are bilingual
We know double the words,
We have double the fun,
But our moms say we are
Double trouble!

Gianna   Julio   Steph

MY BILINGUAL FRIENDS

It's never too early or too late to learn a new language, or to grow your first language. We are all language learners for life.

LANGUAGE LEARNING ACROSS TIME

People first began to learn languages by speaking and listening. They may also have used pictures and paintings.

Then, over time, people in ancient times started to use written forms of language, so people could learn how to read and write languages too.

The El Castillo cave paintings in Spain are over 40,000 years old.

About 1,000 years ago, the first books were printed using printing blocks in China, experts think.

But in many parts of the world, early books were handwritten and had no pages.

Egyptians used reed pens to write.

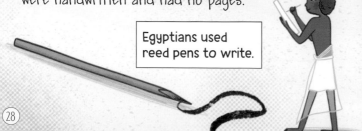

Writing on a clay tablet

Thousands of years ago, pupils learned how to write on tablets of clay in Babylon. The earliest written language was found in China on pottery from about 7,000 years ago.

About 500 years ago, the first printing press was made and used in Germany. The press meant more books could be produced, so more people could learn to read.

Hundreds of years ago, it was mainly boys from rich families who were allowed to study, and it was usually with a private teacher.

Edward VI became king of England when he was nine years old. He had the best private teachers. He learned to read and write English and spoke five other languages.

Edward VI 1536–1553

Sor Juana Inés de la Cruz lived with her mother and grandfather in Mexico. She learned to read when she was just three years old. She studied privately, because girls were not allowed to go to school. By the time she was 13 years old, she was teaching Latin to other children.

In some parts of the world, such as Spain, Italy, and Sweden, girls were allowed to go to school from the 1500s.

But in many other countries, girls and children who weren't from wealthy families were not allowed to go to school.

Even now, not all children can go to school in their countries to learn to read and write languages.

HOW DO WE LEARN NOW?

Today many pupils can learn language anytime, anyplace, anywhere using digital technology. We learn language in a variety of different ways.

How do you like to learn?
How do you learn best?

DIFFERENT LANGUAGES HAVE DIFFERENT WORDS AND MEANINGS

We may say words in different ways even if the language is the same.
How do you say the word *tomato*?
In British English, people say *tom-ar-toe*.
In American English, people say *toe-may-toe*.

We may use different words for the same object in the same language. Do you say *pop* or *soda*?

I speak English. I say *tomato*.

I speak Italian. I say *pomodoro*. It means *golden apple*.

We may use different languages to describe the same idea.

- He's a party animal. (English)
- He's a party lion. (German)
- He's a party gnome. (Swedish)
- He's a party monkey. (Danish)
- He's a little dog of all weddings. (Mexican Spanish)

How do you describe someone like this?

Some languages have words and meanings that do not exist in other languages.

JAPANESE: *KOMOREBI*
The sunlight that shines through the leaves of trees

GERMAN: *WALDEINSAMKEIT*
The feeling of being alone in the woods

RUSSIAN: *POCHEMUCHKA*
A person who asks a lot of questions

HAWAIIAN: *PANAPO'O*
When you scratch your head to help you to remember something

INDONESIAN: *JAYUS*
A bad joke told badly but is funny

Do you have any words like this in your language?

ITALIAN: *CULACCINO*
The mark left on a table by a cold glass

WHAT'S IN A NAME?

Names are an important part of our language and culture. Names are usually very special to us. In most languages, people have first and last names. Some people have one or more other names too.

OSRIC BAKER

OSRIC WOOD

Long ago, people often only had a first name.

If two people had the same name, then their job or where they lived was used to tell them apart.

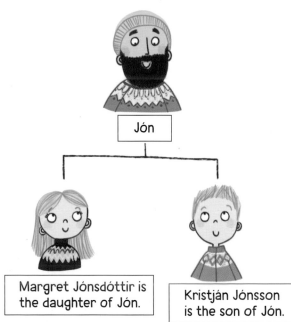

In Iceland, some children are traditionally named as the son or daughter of someone.

Jón

Margret Jónsdóttir is the daughter of Jón.

Kristján Jónsson is the son of Jón.

So, the last name *Wood* might be used by someone who cuts trees for lumber. That is one of the reasons why so many last, or family, names are names of jobs or places.

All over the world, children are sometimes given the same first name as their parents or grandparents as a sign of tradition, respect, or remembrance.

JUCARI is ten and lives with his family in Mexico City. His family belong to a group of indigenous people called the Purépecha, and his name has a special meaning: *great wise one*.

MURK is seven and lives with her family in Pakistan. Her name means *smile*, and it describes her well.

WHAT ABOUT NICKNAMES?

They can be pet names for people, places, or teams.

CHUCK for Charles

CHICKPEA for a small child

CUBBIES for the Chicago Cubs baseball team

THE PEACH STATE for Georgia

Naiyarat is from Thailand. His nickname is **KNIGHT!** Knight lives with his parents, who are teachers, his aunt, Nualrat, and grandma, Rattanapon. Knight likes spending time with his family.

NUALRAT AUNT

AKARAT FATHER

WALEERAT MOTHER

RATTANAPON GRANDMOTHER

KNIGHT

YOUR LANGUAGE AND WHAT MATTERS

Language represents people. It is part of culture and identity. Culture is the way of life that a group of people share. Identity is how you see yourself and your place in the world. So, language is very important to who you are. It is linked to where your family comes from and where you live! Read about these children and how their languages are part of their culture and identity.

NORTH AMERICA

LUKASI is ten years old and lives in Kuujjuaq, in Quebec, Canada. His first language is Inuktitut, but English and French are the national languages of Canada, so he can choose one of those to learn at school too.

SOUTH AMERICA

BASSMA is eight years old. She lives in a village in Morocco. Her family are Berbers—an ancient group of people from North Africa who speak the language Tashelhit. Knowing Tashelhit is an important part of her culture and identity. Standard Moroccan Berber and Moroccan Arabic are national languages, so she also knows those, and some French too.

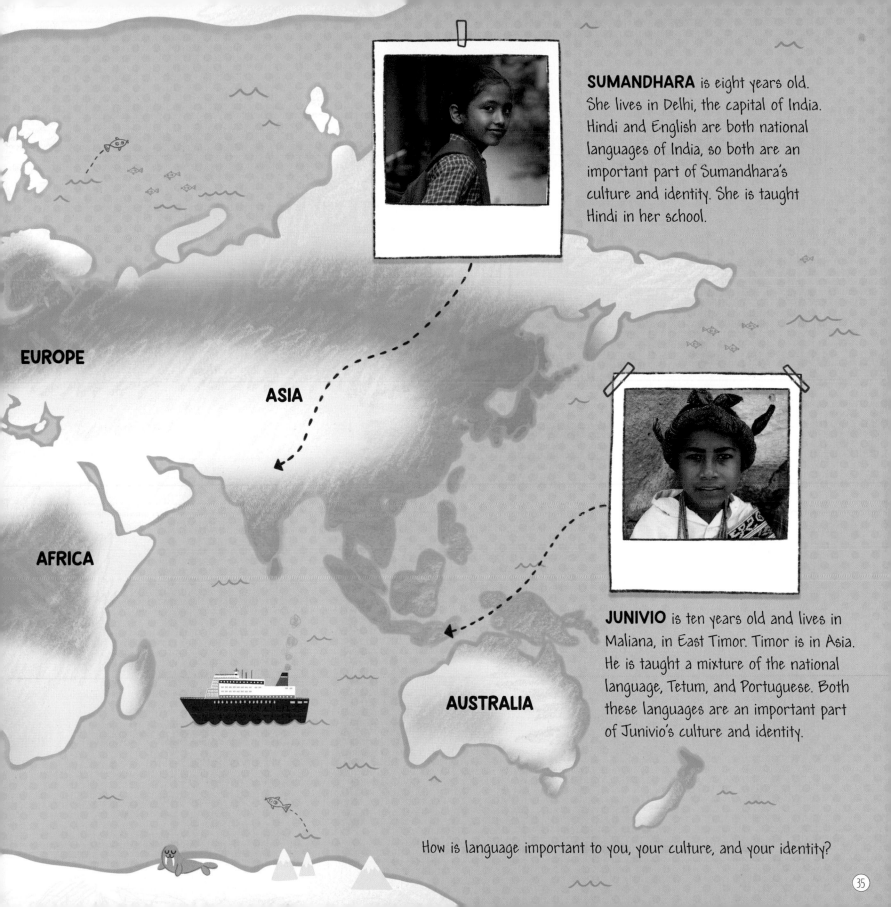

SUMANDHARA is eight years old. She lives in Delhi, the capital of India. Hindi and English are both national languages of India, so both are an important part of Sumandhara's culture and identity. She is taught Hindi in her school.

EUROPE

ASIA

AFRICA

AUSTRALIA

JUNIVIO is ten years old and lives in Maliana, in East Timor. Timor is in Asia. He is taught a mixture of the national language, Tetum, and Portuguese. Both these languages are an important part of Junivio's culture and identity.

How is language important to you, your culture, and your identity?

MUSIC, ART, AND PERFORMANCE

Language is at the core of understanding and communication, but music, art, and performance can be powerful ways to communicate too. Sometimes these forms of communication capture feelings and stories even better than just using words.

Some musicians write set musical pieces that have no words, but express feelings, or tell stories.

Peter and the Wolf, written in 1936 by Sergei Prokofiev, is a story about a boy walking in a meadow. He meets a little bird, a duck, a cat—and a dangerous wolf. A different musical instrument is played to represent each animal Peter meets.

Artists create art to communicate their way of seeing the world, share their emotions, or tell a story.

They use things such as color, types of materials, white space, patterns, and symbols to communicate.

In *Peter and the Wolf*, the French horn represents the wolf.

Barbara Hepworth (1903–1975) made bronze sculptures to represent feelings.

Performance arts are often based on telling stories through movement or gesture.

Puppets can represent characters in stories. The dragon is a symbol of good luck in Chinese New Year celebrations and an important character in ancient Chinese stories. The puppet helps to retell the story while dancing through the streets.

There are many types of dance, and each has its own language.

Kathakali is a dance form from Kerala, in southern India. Kathakali means *story-play*. The dancer uses facial expressions and hand gestures to tell traditional stories.

You have to look at art, listen to music, and watch performing arts carefully—especially those with no spoken words—to understand the language.

CODES

Codes can be pictures, words, letters, symbols, and numbers. The pictures, words, letters, symbols, and numbers are used like language to communicate. What do codes communicate?

Some codes are instructions.

Computers have their own languages, and people called coders learn those languages so they can write instructions called algorithms. The algorithms are the instructions to program machines.

For example, programming a robot to put on a pair of socks might follow this simple algorithm.

Step 1: Locate the sock

Step 2: Pick up the sock

Step 3: Place sock on one foot

Step 4: Repeat steps 1-3 for other foot

A B C D E F G

H I J K L M N

O P Q R S T U

V W X Y Z

Some codes are part of languages and help people to communicate.

Braille was inspired by a code called night writing. It was a way to help soldiers communicate silently at night. Louis Braille developed that code into braille in 1824.

Braille is a system of reading and writing for people who are blind or cannot see well. It is made up of little bumps and dots that are like a code and represent letters and numbers.

Sign language—which is used by and with people who are deaf or hard of hearing, or who cannot speak—mainly uses hand gestures that are like a code.

EAT	DRINK	MORE	THANK YOU	SORRY

Some codes are made to be tricky. Tricky codes can be fun.

Tricky codes can be good for keeping secrets. Julius Caesar was a Roman leader more than 2,000 years ago. He used a code to keep secrets from other leaders he was fighting. His code made each letter of the alphabet match to a different letter of the alphabet. Can you crack these words in code?: fwem and ewrecmg.

…W X Y Z Ⓐ B C D E F G H I J K L M N O P Q R S T U V…

…W X Ⓨ Z A B C D E F G H I J K L M N O P Q R S T U V…

Some ancient languages are like tricky codes. This very old Greek writing is a code that has never been cracked. We do not know what it says or means.

39

ANIMAL TALK

Animals don't have words like humans do, but many animals use sounds and actions to communicate. Experts have "decoded" a lot of animal communication, but there is still plenty more to try to understand.

COMMUNICATING WITH SOUNDS

Birds may sing to mark their territory. They may sing to attract a partner.

Monkeys and baboons may screech to communicate danger.

Bears, tigers, and lions growl to show their fear or strength.

Male humpback whales sing. They make squeals, whistles, and low gurgles to tell other whales they are near. They moan, howl, and cry for a long time.

COMMUNICATING WITH ACTIONS

Rabbits and hares thump their back legs to communicate danger.

Bees dance to tell other bees where there are flowers.

Dogs bow down on their front legs to communicate that they want to play. They wag their tails to show excitement.

Some male birds show their tails to attract a partner.

LEARN SHARK BODY TALK

Sharks do not talk or make sounds. But sharks seem to use their bodies to communicate with each other.

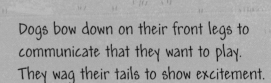

Splashing can mean, *Stay away from my food!*

Hunching can mean, *Stay away from me!*

Swimming by can mean, *Do I know you?*

Circling can mean, *Can I eat before you?*

LANGUAGE RECORD BREAKERS AND COOL FACTS

Read these amazing facts about languages. Catch them quickly because they might change!

1.13 BILLION TOTAL SPEAKERS

WHICH ARE THE THREE MOST SPOKEN LANGUAGES IN THE WORLD?

English has about 1.13 billion total speakers. Mandarin Chinese has about the same. Hindi has about 615 million total speakers.

Hello
(hell-low)

नमस्ते
(nuh-muh-stay)

你好
(nee-how)

840 LANGUAGES

WHICH COUNTRY HAS THE MOST LANGUAGES?

Papua New Guinea has the most languages. It is an island country in the Pacific Ocean, and 840 languages are spoken there.

37 OFFICIAL LANGUAGES

WHICH COUNTRY HAS THE MOST OFFICIAL LANGUAGES?

Bolivia has the most official languages. Official languages are those used by the government. Bolivia has 37 official languages.

WHY DO WE CALL IT AN ALPHABET?

The word *alphabet* comes from the first two letters of the Greek alphabet: *alpha* and *beta*!

Aα
Bβ

74 CHARACTERS

WHICH LANGUAGE HAS THE LONGEST ALPHABET?

The Cambodian language Khmer has the longest alphabet with 74 characters. Cambodia is a country in Asia.

(key) (tiger)

(car) (salt)

11 LETTERS

WHICH LANGUAGE HAS THE SHORTEST ALPHABET?

The Papuan language Rotokas has the shortest alphabet with just 11 letters.

a, b, e, g, i, k, o, p, r, t, u

250,000 WORDS

WHICH LANGUAGE HAS THE MOST WORDS?

English has the most words with more than 250,000.

What were the first words spoken by a human in space?

The Earth is blue. How wonderful. It is amazing.

Yuri Gagarin, Russian astronaut, 1961

That's one small step for man, one giant leap for mankind.

What were the first words spoken from the surface of the moon?

Neil Armstrong, American astronaut, 1969

Mr. Watson, come here. I want to see you.

What were the first words spoken on the telephone?

Alexander Graham Bell, inventor of the telephone, 1876

A VISUAL ROADMAP OF LANGUAGE

Explore some of the amazing facts about language from this book.

REMEMBER!
Catch them quickly because language is constantly evolving.

ABOUT 4,700 YEARS OLD: Egyptian is the oldest ancient language still spoken today. Modern-day Egyptian, Coptic, is used in the north of East Africa, and it is not written in hieroglyphs anymore.

REMEMBER!
Most languages belong to one of the 142 language families of the world.

REMEMBER!
All languages are meaningful. You just have to explore the language to find the meaning!

PREHISTORY (BEFORE RECORDS BEGAN): Humans living about 2.5 million years ago may have communicated with grunts and signs.

ABOUT 400,000 YEARS AGO: The hyoid bone is found in the neck of ancient, fossilized humans. It is a bone that allows humans to speak rather than grunt. It tells us that those ancient people could probably speak using words similar to the way we do now.

REMEMBER!
Different languages have different symbols to stand for letters or words.

OVER 2,000 YEARS AGO: Latin was once spoken in the Roman Empire.

REMEMBER!
Languages become extinct if people stop using them.

REMEMBER!
Some languages today are spoken languages—such as Pirahã, which is spoken by the Pirahã people of Brazil, South America.

FIRST RECORDS OF WRITTEN LANGUAGE ABOUT 7,000 YEARS AGO: The earliest written language was found in China on pottery. It was a form of writing called cuneiform. Thin wooden sticks with triangular ends were pressed into wet clay.

OVER 1,000 YEARS AGO: The Vikings spoke Old Norse. Over time, words from Old Norse mixed with Old English spoken in Britain to create a new variation of English.

OLDEST CAVE PAINTINGS FROM ABOUT 40,000 YEARS AGO: The El Castillo cave paintings in Spain.

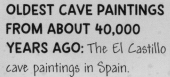

REMEMBER!
Languages move and change over time, just like people do!

Edward VI (**1500s**) was learning languages with a private tutor.

The first Apple App Store was launched, **2008**.

The word *app* is named "word of the year" by the American Dialect Society, **2010**.

REMEMBER!
About 96 percent of the world's primary-school-aged children go to school in their countries to learn to read and write languages. But that means 4 percent are not so lucky.

Sor Juana Inés de la Cruz (**1600s**), aged 13, was teaching Latin to children.

Apps shifted from fun games and social media to more lifestyle focused— including language learning and translations.

HUNDREDS OF YEARS AGO:
It was mainly boys from rich families who were allowed to study, and it was usually with a private teacher.

First words spoken on a telephone, **1876**.

The first iPhone was released, **2007**.

LANGUAGE WILL ALWAYS BE:
About communication.

About speaking, listening, reading, and writing— and body language too!

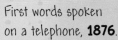

Mr. Watson, come here, I want to see you.

Google Translate launched, **2006**.

Alexander Graham Bell, inventor of the telephone.

REMEMBER!
Printing books was faster, so more people could learn to read from a book.

LAST CENTURY:
Computer technology began to develop.

THIS CENTURY AND ONWARD:
Clearer links between technology and language begin to develop.

REMEMBER!
Music, art, performance arts, and codes can be used like language to communicate.

Language is something most people learn from very early on in life.

Our language systems are evolving, and our writing systems are almost impossible to preserve ... so we really have no idea what language will be in the future, and what people of the future will make of it.

ABOUT 500 YEARS AGO:
The first printing press was made and used in Germany.

OVER 70 YEARS AGO:
The first programmable electronic computer was in use, **1948**.

OVER 60 YEARS AGO:
The first automated language translation system, which translated 250 words between Russian and English, **1954**.

The oldest computer programming language, Fortran, was in use and is still in use today, **1957**.

ABOUT 1,000 YEARS AGO:
Experts think that the first books were printed using printing blocks in China.

The first Guinness World Records book was published, **1955**. It has been translated into more than 22 languages.

WORKING WITH LANGUAGE

There are many ways to work with language or languages. For some jobs, such as being a translator, it is essential that you know multiple languages so that you can do the job. For other jobs, such as being a customer service worker, having more than one language means you can help more people, but it isn't essential. For some jobs, like being a field researcher, you might choose to learn another language or pick it up as part of the job.

LANGUAGE TEACHER
studies languages in order to teach them.

LINGUIST
studies languages or can speak them very well.

EDITOR
selects or revises content for publication.

TRANSLATOR
changes what someone has written from one language into another.

INTERPRETER
changes what someone is saying into the words of another language.

INTERNATIONAL DEVELOPMENT WORKER
provides help to communities in the developing world and often in emergency situations. It's helpful if they can speak the language of those in need.

BROADCAST JOURNALIST
researches, investigates, and presents news for television, radio, and online. It's helpful if they can speak in the language of those they are interviewing.

TOUR GUIDE
shows tourists around places and explains what is important to look at and know.

FIELD RESEARCHER
collects information to understand how people or communities interact. They generally use the information for business development.

INTELLIGENCE ROLE
works for a government and listens in on conversations in other countries to try to understand or stop any harmful events being planned. It's kind of like being a spy!

CUSTOMER SERVICE
talks and supports customers in a business. It's helpful if they can speak the customers' language.

AUTHOR
writes content for publication in print or online.

INDEX

GLOSSARY

PAGES	WORD	MEANING
pp4–5	communicate	the speaker and listener must understand one another for communication to occur. Communication requires understanding. Language is our attempt to foster that.
	gesture	a movement of the body, hands, arms, or head to express an idea or feeling
	extinct	no longer active
	official language	the language or one of the languages that is accepted by a country's government, is taught in schools, used in the courts of law, etc.
	bilingual	someone who speaks or uses two languages
	multilingual	someone who speaks or uses more than two languages
pp6–7	volume	how loudly you are speaking
	tone	the way you say something and how it can change the meaning

PAGES	WORD	MEANING
pp12–13	coo	to speak in a soft, gentle, or loving way
	babble	to talk or say something that has no meaning
pp16–17	evolve	to develop gradually over time
pp28–29	printing press	a machine for printing text or pictures from type or plates
pp32–33	lumber	wood that has been prepared for building
pp34–35	culture	the way of life that a group of people share
	identity	how you see yourself and your place in the world
pp40–41	territory	an area that an animal or person tries to control or thinks belongs to them
	hunching	to bend your back into a round shape
pp44–45	programmable	used to describe a computer or machine that is able to accept instructions to do a range of tasks, rather than just one